YOU CAN MAKE YOUR LIFE
BEAUTIFUL

Discover a Simple Path to Happiness

BO SANCHEZ

SHEPHERD'S
V O I C E

YOU CAN MAKE
YOUR LIFE
BEAUTIFUL

YOU CAN MAKE
YOUR LIFE
BEAUTIFUL
Discover a Simple Path to Happiness

BO SANCHEZ

A *KERYGMA* Collection Book
SHEPHERD'S VOICE

Requests for information should be addressed to:
SHEPHERD'S VOICE Publications, Inc.
60 Chicago St., Cubao, Quezon City 1109 Philippines
Tel. No. (02) 411-7874
Fax No. (02) 727-5615
E-mail: sale-svp@philonline.com.ph

Layout design by Noli Vicedo

ISBN-971-91756-4-8

The stories in this book first appeared in KERYGMA magazine under
the column, *The BOss* by Bo Sanchez.

Dearest Marowe,
every time I watch you smile,
I'm reminded of two things:
that God plays favorites,
and I am one of them.

Thank you for making my life beautiful.

Contents

Preface

The title of this book is my dream for you.

You can make your life beautiful.

Because deep down, beneath the mess of your problems, it already is beautiful.

Because all the happiness that you need for your soul is found within you.

Take my hand now.

Walk with me and join me in my sometimes funny, sometimes crazy journeys.

If in one story, you discover a spiritual truth that will raise the quality of your life, or give you deeper joy, or change the direction of your path—then hold on to that truth. Stop reading and loiter for a while until you've embraced that gem of wisdom. Make it your own. Baptize it with your name. If you do this, you will find that truth leading you to create wonderful things, pointing to areas of your soul that need repair and realignment.

And when you feel that you're ready, walk with me on to the next story.

Be as beautiful as God wants you to be.

KEEP THE NUMBER
OF YOUR HEART SECRET

Can you believe this?

At a time when *KERYGMA*[1] had about 250,000 readers all over the country (there's more today)— plus a few more thousands around the world, we only had two phone lines in our office.

You read that right: Two.

That was like putting the entire Pacific Ocean through a small two-inch pipe.

And rusty ones, too. Because our phones had the audacity to break down on us. During that memorable era of our history, if you called us up—and heard a ring—you didn't shout Yabadabadoo just yet. Some actually danced the boogie and bought some ice cream at that point, but we advised not to do them yet.

Because the phone could have been busted, and all you'd have heard was the ringing. And the ringing. And the ringing. And nothing else, except your own scream: *"Aaaarrrrgggggggh!"* Imagine how our callers felt? Some suffered a neurotic episode right there.

And if you heard a ring when you called us up, we asked people to check what time it was: It may have been two in the morning.

But here was the real miracle. If you finally heard our receptionist lift up the receiver and say, *"This is KERYGMA office, may I help you?"* we gave you the go ahead signal to break down into joyful weeping and dance not only the boogie, but the cha-cha and tango at the same time. Buy the ice cream we told you, and fly off to Boracay.

Because you beat the odds.

You won.

You out-dialed thousands of callers.

Believe me, probability-wise, you had more chances of being killed by a terrorist than reaching us by phone.

Guess what.

Nowadays, I feel that God doesn't eat ice cream as often as He wants to.

Because every time He calls us, all He gets is the busy signal.

Our hearts receive thousands of calls from our different affections and attachments and ambitions...

This is my suggestion (It's really quite simple): *Keep the number of your heart secret.* Between you and God. Please don't share it to the whole world. *Let your deepest, most powerful affections be for Him. Alone.*

And then no one else will clog your line.

Not your dreams.

Or your idols.

Or your other loves.

God isn't on a diet.

Let Him enjoy all the ice cream in the world.

---

[1] Kerygma is one of the most widely read Catholic inspirational magazines in the Philippines.

YOU CAN MAKE YOUR LIFE BEAUTIFUL

I hold her hand.

And stroke her hair gently.

And getting enough courage, I steal a kiss from her cheek.

And when she finally smiles at me, I think I am one incredibly lucky guy.

Tracy is already a young woman.

But her head is bent downward, and drool flows through one side of her mouth, and her face is bereft of any expression. She can't speak. Or move by herself. Every once in a while, someone has to shift the position of her head, her arms, her legs—or else they become painfully sore. (Doctors regularly give her painkillers.)

And the hand I hold is small for her age and contorted. Her limbs are terribly thin, twisted, and abnormally short, and have to be strapped in a special wheelchair.

She doesn't eat the way you and I do. She's fed through a tube attached straight through her abdomen.

Some would call her a vegetable.

I wouldn't. Because her name is Tracy.[1]

And there's one thing she does well, despite all these.

Tracy smiles.

And her smile takes your breath away.

You see, she is able to smile when she likes something.

It's the only way she communicates.

So I playfully rub the back of her neck, and whisper to her ear, *"Tracy, do you like this? Smile if you do..."*

She does, and it's so sweet, you'd fall in love with her right there. I wipe her saliva with her bib, which is now soaking wet, and continue to hold her hand for the rest of the day.

I go home with tears in my eyes.

The next morning, I visit her again.

I can't get away.

Yes, I know the past days were the most unproductive days of my life: no articles written, no preaching made, no songs composed, no meetings held, no books read, no plans designed...

All I did was hold her hand.

And allowed myself to be loved by a smile.

But the peace I felt!

And I realize why: I was being deeply transformed by the power of this girl—the one who couldn't even move a finger.

Tracy was training my soul to love well. She was training me to love one person, one face, one heart at a time. And she was training me to find love in the most unexpected places.

Even her memory speaks to me, asking me to slow

down if I want to really love.

I picture her in my mind, and she smiles.

She tells me that I always have a choice.

I can make life beautiful.

---

[1] Tracy lives in *Daybreak, L'arche* community in Canada, a special home for the mentally handicapped.

HUG SOMEONE TODAY, WHILE THERE'S TIME

*M*y father isn't the expressive, sentimental type. He isn't the hugging, *"I love you"* kind of a guy.

But I recall as a young boy, he showed his love to me the only way he knew best: He spent enormous time with me. We'd jog together every night, walk to a pizza joint on weekends, and simply talk. (Actually, I'd do the talking and he'd do the listening.)

My father was my best friend.

A few months ago, Dad was trying to fix a light bulb in our garage. Standing onto a chair for greater reach, he lost his balance and went crashing down. His head hit the concrete floor and immediately, blood spurted out like water from an open faucet.

Because of the impact, there was like a dripping faucet inside his brain as well. Blood clots started to appear in his X-rays, and he began to experience paralysis in his body. Even after brain surgery, he lost his language ability because of a new blood clot, found even deeper than the others—too deep for another surgery to reach.

The gravest blow was severe pneumonia, an infection that developed after a few months of staying in the hospital. His lungs were now filled with fluid, and that was when the crisis hit.

He was hooked up to a respirator, and the long

wait began: The doctors told us frankly that he could go anytime. At that point, he was only absorbing 20% of the oxygen they were pumping into him. Someone doesn't last too long in that state.

I looked at Dad's hands and face, and they were bluish in color. I whispered to his ear, *"I love you, Dad."*

That was when he regained consciousness for a few minutes. He looked at me with so much sadness in his eyes.

Then he did something that he never did in my entire life. He raised his hands towards my face, and clasped me on both cheeks. Then he brought me down towards him, and gave me a hug.

My father gave me a hug.

He was telling me that he loved me, too.

He was also probably bidding farewell.

My emotions were running wild inside me.

I was both grieving and joyful.

Joyful because for the first time, my tough, unsentimental father gave me a hug. Grieving because he was going away. Grieving because it might be the last hug I'll ever get from him.

"Dad, we should have done this a long time ago," I muttered to myself.

Today, my father has recovered a little bit, narrowly escaping that ordeal.

I hug him more often now.

Hug someone today, while there's time.

YOUR PAST DOESN'T DEFINE YOUR FUTURE

I can still see it.

There was a bamboo hut I saw while traveling in a far-flung island in the country. Right smack in the middle of nowhere, with mountain ranges and farmlands around it, lay this tiny shack the size of your regular toilet.

I had to stop to take a good look, because it had a sign on top of it. And the sign was bigger than the house itself. I read it, in big, bold, bright, red letters:

**GLOBAL OUTREACH FOR JESUS
(INTERNATIONAL)**

Now they'd be in trouble if that were their central office.

Then boy, whoever put that sign had faith.

I actually felt like that bamboo hut when at fourteen years old, a prayer group leader "prophesied" to me that I will preach to different nations all over the world.

She said she had heard God tell her that in her prayers.

Wow!

Me, an international preacher.

Ha!

I'm *not* insane, thank you.

You see, I knew myself. I saw who I was every

time I looked at the mirror, which I tried to avoid to relieve myself of unnecessary stress. I was a small-packaged, toothpick-structured, pimple-infested, grotesquely-formed, fourteen-year-old creature—who also wasn't very bright. I was struggling in high school algebra, chemistry, physics, and Pilipino.

I wasn't much of anything, really.

Oh, I was a preacher all right.

At that time, I was already leading a small prayer group of thirty (30) people. Impressed? Don't be. My audience was um... a little bit biased. The regular members of my prayer group were the following: my mother, my father, my five sisters, their husbands, my nieces, my aunts, their husbands, my cousins, and the neighborhood dogs. Count that and you get thirty very loyal people with a few representatives from the animal kingdom.

International Preacher?

Lunacy.

But listen. I'm now thirty-three years old. With lesser pimples, but with a receding hairline now. (I don't run out of problems.)

And the insane has happened: I've preached to sooooo many nations all over the world these past years, I sometimes wonder if my next flight will be to a planet called Jupiter.

I'm not boasting. You see, I don't think I can. Ever.

I still see myself as that bamboo hut out in the middle of nowhere. I'm still that fourteen-year-old nobody.

All it had to take was God.

And a guy who failed in algebra, physics, and chemistry.

The truth?

Your past doesn't define your future.

MAKE GOD YOUR HOME

I've been traveling too much, I sometimes wake up in the morning wondering what city I'm in. Am I in Davao? Or Bacolod? Or Toronto? Or L.A.? Or Jakarta? Or Cebu? Everything is a giant blur.

But the moment I step outside the sunny day, and inhale the heavy, poisonous, potent, mutant, radioactive, genetically-altering, tuberculosis-causing, cancer-inducing fumes of the air...

Ahhh... (Cough.)

Instantly, I know I'm back in Manila.

This is *my* city.

Where else are you forced to trust God every time you inhale? Only here.

And many people complain of its absurd, insane, foolish traffic jam. It's phenomenal how we cause them, I think it'll become one of our major tourist attractions.

But I call it *sweet* traffic. This monstrosity causes me to do an extra fifteen decades of the rosary in the car. Cool, hmm?

While doing so, I try to avoid a mad rush of death-machines swerving left and right beside me (I think they were called public buses decades ago). I say a prayer for the crazy drivers, *"Father forgive them, for they do not know what they are doing..."* My patience is tested and stretched, and little by little, my soul gets love-trained for Heaven.

And when I walk through Megamall [1], and see the crowd that rivals the sands of Pinatubo—it becomes the perfect place for earnest intercession. I walk around, praying for that happy couple eating ice cream, that crying child on her mother's breast, that bored saleslady, that punkish kid...

I pray for hundreds of people during those days.

Suddenly, God becomes very close to me.

If given a choice, I can decide to live somewhere else—tomorrow if need be. I can escape it all and move to a tiny hamlet in a remote island of the Philippines.

I'd escape the heat, the smog, the madness...

But deep in my heart, I believe God wants me here.

In Manila.

This is my mission place.

And my home is where God is.

And He's here.

I feel Him in every breath I take. (Cough.)

Listen. Any place can be your home. It's not the location. Or the ambiance. Or the scenery. It's where God is calling you, pure and simple.

Do you feel Him where you are?

If not, *you're not yet home.*

---

[1] The biggest shopping mall in Manila

GOD WILL MEET YOU WHERE YOU ARE

I'm taking post-graduate courses in Theology to remind me of how ignorant I really am. You see, I love listening to my brilliant professors speak high-tech "theologese."

But I guess it's not just for me. I can't write straight with big, heavy-duty words, quoting stuff from super-duper theologians.

That work to me is just a little bit less difficult than doing advanced Trigonometry. But I recall one time when I took a shot at it. I started pounding on the keyboard, *"Some contemporary approaches to spirituality convey paradigmatic alterations from traditional soteriology, rooted in modern Biblical hermeneutics..."*

Ugh... It was pure torture. (I offered my sufferings for the conversion of the world. And I bet you'd do that, too, if I wrote that way, hmm?)

But in all this, I've learned something quite glorious:

God is flexible.

He's made of rubber.

He can stoop down to hollow, lazy brains like mine.

And He can also meet the best and sharpest minds of big-time theologians. And still win.

He can be wise to the wise.

And simple to the simple.

I've realized that God will meet us where we are.

He can be very tender to you if you need an embrace.

He can be firm to you if you need some spanking.

He can be terribly awesome when you need a miracle.

He can be painfully quiet when He wants you to trust Him.

He will be what you need him to be.

(Note: Not *"want"* Him to be. I said, *"need"* Him to be.)

Question: What do you really need right now?

Believe me.

He knows about it more than you do.

So let Him meet you where you are.

And let Him love you, right there.

LET SOME THINGS
NOT CHANGE

I remember a time when life was a little simpler.

During an ancient, pre-historic era, there was only one *Shakey's* pizza store in the country—located in far away Angeles City. I was only twelve years old when my father would bring me there for a two-hour drive, just to eat pizza. He'd eat two slices, and I'd eat the rest.

More than the pizza, however, I treasure the time I spent with Dad. In my heart, I knew that my father loved me. *Because he loved me enough to waste his time on me.*

Things have changed now. Today, we no longer go out of town to eat pizza. We don't even have to leave the house. I just dial delivery, and Dad and I can eat pizza. My father's an older man now, and so am I (Sniffle). Sometimes, I pay the bill. (Waaaah!)

But when I really think about it, the *deeper things* haven't changed. Dad still eats two slices, and I still eat the rest. And I still enjoy his deep friendship, much more than ever.

As a kid, Dad and I walked together to Cubao, and we loved passing by that tiny Shoemart (SM)—if you can still remember—that ancient SM that sold only shoes and nothing else.

I loved those walks!

Just Dad and me, walking man to man.

What has changed?

Today, SM consumes about 30% of the geographical land space of the Republic of the Philippines. And it sells everything else except nuclear reactors and live piranha.

Also, Dad and I are no longer able to take long walks. I've become a missionary and that has taken me away from home. But when given a chance, I invite Dad and Mom to hop along the journey. So we've gone together to different parts of the world.

They don't give talks or anything like that.

I still do the preaching. But from the pulpit, I could see Dad and Mom, praying at the back of the crowd.

They're praying for *me.*

They love me.

Thank God, some things don't ever change.

Because in this insanely chaotic world of ours, our kids desperately need to know that they can hold on to certain realities that *remain true for life.*

Or else they'll lose their way, and die somewhere inside.

HOLD HANDS

*B*oy and girl.
Sweet young things.
Around their late teens.
Both walking in front of me, lost in their world of cute cupids, beating hearts, and chocolate cream cakes with caramel toppings.
They walk as if walking on air, hand in hand.
Hip to hip.
Shoulder to shoulder.
Eye to eye.
Nose to nose.
Bad breath to bad breath.
But do they mind?
Of course not. They're in *luv.*
I watch this scene with amusement one night, while going home from one prayer meeting.
At my side was another couple walking home.
Friends of mine.
Not so young.
With three kids. (The eldest is twenty-three years old.)
Grandparents in the making, really.
In fact, the guy's balding. There's nothing on top except a few overstaying weeds. Airplanes can land in and out without a problem. He can sing *Shine*,

Jesus, Shine with superb visual effects. He compensates by his bushy eyebrows, combing them upwards as far as possible.

The woman on the other hand is gifted, endowed, and abundant. Through her, the vastness of the Kingdom is displayed. She has cellulite deposits with interest compounded daily. Indeed, she receives all that life has to offer her. And to her embarrassment, people always ask her, *"When are you giving birth?"*

But this fiftyish couple does something that blows my mind.

They walk hand in hand as well.

And their handholding is so different from the way the young lovebirds in front of me hold hands.

This time, I know it isn't just a cutey-sweety symbol. It's proven. Full. Real. Unquestionable. Pregnant! (With meaning!) Backed up by twenty-five years of cooking meals, washing dishes, doing the laundry, and raising bratty kids.

Stop reading. And hold the hand of your spouse. Your mom. Your dad. Your friend. And prove it for the next twenty-five years.

And beyond.

KNOW YOUR DEEPEST DESIRES

*W*hen I was getting married, I cried *"Heeeeeeeeelp!"* I wanted to call the Fire Brigade. The Marines! The SWAT team. Power Rangers! Batman and Robin. Lois and Clark! Jacky Chan. Anybody!

Why?

Because I felt incredibly awkward.

To say *"I was getting married,"* was like as saying, *"I'm blonde"* or *"I'm from Pluto"* or *"My nose is gorgeous."* Because if you've been reading stuff I wrote a few years back, you'd probably recall these lines from me:

"My friends, I want to remain celibate for life. Will He give me the grace to remain so? I'm giving myself two years to pray for the blessing of celibacy. If I find it, and I really hope I do, I'll make a more permanent decision at that time..."

Well, that was written in December of 1995.

And I didn't find the grace. Sniffle.

I prayed for the gift of celibacy.

He gave me the gift of marriage instead.

(Mom, don't cry too much. My son may be a bishop.)

In this whole discernment process about my future, I realized two important things about me.

1) I love being a lay preacher. I love it too much to

give it up for a roman collar and velvet stole and church altar. Preaching as a normal human being works too well for me.

2) My heart longs for a female companion too much, too often, too strongly. What can I say? I'm made for *luv*. (Oh no! I'm watching too many Meg Ryan movies.)

A friend of mine tells me that searching for the will of God "out there" is a big boo-boo. Because His will for us is in the depths of our hearts. We'll discover His plan for our lives in our DEEPEST DESIRES. (Still, it'll take prayer and time to find out what they are!) When God made us, He implanted within us a burning desire for His will. He'll never twist our arm and say, *"Be a priest!"* or *"Be a nun!"* or *"Get married!"* or *"Be the Tom Cruise of the Philippines."*

He won't force.

Because we'll simply desire His will.

Period.

SAY 'THANK YOU' OFTEN

When I was a kid, I sort of liked getting sick. Honest.

Not only because I could miss school and stay home. I liked being sick because Mom would bring me milk and cookies as I stayed in bed.

In all the times I got sick as a kid (which was about every other month), I never saw my Mom get too tired not to serve me, or feed me, or fuss over me. In my mind, the earth may shake, the moon melt, and the sun explode, but she was the one thing in this universe that will never ever change.

Many years later, already as a lay missionary, I remember getting terribly sick. And there she was, just as if the decades folded up into mere days, as she went up to my room for her hourly visits, bringing food, warm clothes, medicine, prayer, etc. Again, it felt good having a loving mother to watch over me. All I had to do was ask, and she'd be there for me.

But this time, as her visits progressed, I noticed how she entered my room almost panting, her breath short, her words faint, her movements slow. I also read in her eyes the acceptance of a painful loss: for the first time, she was discovering that she couldn't care for me much longer.

My suspicions were right. A few days later, she

tearfully shared with me her emotional realization.

"I'm just getting older, Bo. I get so tired these past few days caring for you. I began thinking that perhaps it'll be good for you to get married and have a wife now." That was the first time she ever said that to me—someone who for years always wanted me to be a priest.

One day, Mom got sick. A rare event when it happens. So I went to her room, sat beside her, and chatted about everything she wanted to talk about. (To her, talking to me is better than all the milk and cookies in the world.) I felt good just being beside her.

I'm writing this to you, Mom.

I know I travel a lot and I'm rarely at home, because that's the life of a missionary. And I do thank you for your all-out support for me in my decision to serve the Lord.

But if you do get sick, and no one's at home to give you milk and cookies, I want you to know that all you have to do is call me, and I'll be there for you. Yes, we can talk as much as you want.

You're the best mother I can ever wish for.

You may be too old to care for me the way you did, but I'm old enough to care for you now.

In my pride, I don't show it as much as I should, but I just want you to know that I love you, Mom.

I really, really do.

You have given me your life.

Thank you.

DO WHAT LOVE DEMANDS

I now own a cell phone.

People who have been reading my stuff for a few years know how I love the simple lifestyle, *ala*-St. Francis of Assisi. I've always wanted an uncluttered and free life. I didn't want ringing, beeping, and vibrating things disturbing my prayer time. And for the sake of humility (or so I thought), I didn't want the status symbol of a cell phone hanging from my belt.

So except for my computer where I write my books, for many years I've avoided all sorts of personal gadgetry, equipment, and other luxuries: no car, no cellular, no beeper, no wristwatch, no walkman, no girlfriend, etc.

But slowly, I had to face harsh reality.

My once friendly, gentle, and otherwise mentally balanced staff of seventy-five people—either working for SHEPHERD'S VOICE (publisher of this book), or my Catholic community, or ANAWIM (our work for the poor)—have become more and more violent these past few months.

I hear screams like, *"Where were you? Planet Mars?! We've been looking all over the world for you these past three days!"* Suicide attempts have been reported to me. A few have been acting weird every time the moon is full. And I have received a few death threats from otherwise very loving people, if I don't get a cell phone.

I've realized that there is *one law above every other law.* Yup, even above my desire for simplicity. Or prayer. Or humility. It's called *the demand of love.*

If I love these people, I'm going to get a cell phone. Whether it'll interfere with my simple lifestyle, my prayer life, and my great humility. (You see, I'm the most humble person in the world. I get awards for my profound humility. You know, I'm so humble that blah, blah, blah, blah, blah...)

What does love demand in your life?

Disturbing your prayer time because your little son wants you to carry him? Not attending your prayer meeting this week because its Mom's birthday? Saying "yes" to a leadership position even if you really want something low-key? Saying "no" to an abusive friend even if everything about you wants to say yes?

For me, it was the simple act of getting a cell phone.

I also got myself a girlfriend who is now my wife, but then, that's another story.

GIVE YOUR HEART AWAY
AND FIND IT WHOLE

I now have six children.

One day, I had zero. The next day, I have six.

No, I don't have six wives that gave birth on the same day.

Last June 1996, I took in six orphans in my little bamboo hut in ANAWIM. Varying in ages, they're siblings whose parents died a few years back.

Taking them was a big mistake.

I ate with these kids, prayed with them, played with them, read them bedtime stories, and whenever I arrived home, they'd hang on to me like I was a Christmas tree.

When we'd finish dinner, I'd hear one of them say, *"Kuya Bo, magbasa ka na tungkol kay Jesus..."*[1]

I recall sitting on the bamboo floor, and the two smallest kids scrambling for my lap, and the older ones standing beside and behind me. I'd read slowly, pointing to the pages of a kid's picture Bible. A thousand questions are asked. They'd laugh, share their simple experiences, and sometimes just listen quietly. In the meantime, the youngest girl would yawn, rest her head on one of my arms, and sleep beautifully. I'd look at her cuddled up on my lap, and I'd tell myself again, *"this is really one big mistake."*

One night, I cried. But they were really tears of

joy. I was realizing that my life was ridiculously changing, right before my eyes. Because whenever I left them to go back to my apartment in Manila, or preach in different parts of the world, I cannot silence the persistent ache within me. It throbs like a hidden wound.

It just takes a sight of a parent carrying his child. Or a toy left on the floor. Or a store selling children's clothes. Immediately, my heart travels a thousand miles away to my bamboo hut in ANAWIM. What are *my* kids doing now?

I miss them terribly.

I miss their noise, their laughter, their smells.

I miss holding that tiny, sleeping girl in my arms.

I must admit. My heart is no longer mine. It has been broken, and its shattered pieces now reside in tiny hearts. They do not know the power they have over me. In their utter helplessness, they now own me. I love them deeply. I've become their prisoner. And I hope I'll never get released.

But ironically, in this shattered condition of my heart, I've never felt so whole. So alive. So free.

Yes, it was a big mistake adopting them.

Probably one of the most beautiful mistakes I've ever made in my life.

---

[1] Brother Bo, please read to us something about Jesus?

AVOID POTHOLES
BY TAKING HUMPS[1]

*T*hey tell me that the average speed of a car in Manila is 25 kph. That's catastrophically slow. That's just the speed of a turtle injected with steroids.

Aside from traffic, there are two other things that make vehicles go slow: humps and potholes.

Between these two, I'd rather choose humps.

Especially those that are painted bright yellow and smooth on the curves, with nice signs to tell us they're coming.

But I don't like potholes, period.

They come in all sizes: tiny Mickey Mouse holes to nuclear bomb testing craters.

And they never come announced. They just appear when you're one inch away, and *kabloom*. And *kablagblagblag...*

Life's like that.

When God wants you to slow down, He'll send you potholes. But He can never give you humps, because that's something that you should deliberately make for youself. (More on this later.)

Potholes are the small and big problems of your life.

When you have a bleeding hangnail, an expensive Italian shoe isn't very beautiful. When your doctor tells you that you have malignant cancer, your

Mercedes or BMW suddenly lacks oomph. And when you discover that your teenage son is on drugs, your jewelry doesn't shine as brilliantly as before.

Like potholes, problems come suddenly. No one warns you they're coming. And your whole life goes *kabloom* and *kablagblagblag...*

But because of these kablooms, you're forced to stop and think. You ask fundamental questions, like, *"What's life all about? Where am I going?"* Overnight, your hierarchy of values changes. The most important things in life—such as your soul, your family, your God—become painfully obvious. And what used to be so pressing and insistent and noisy, reveal themselves to be cheap.

Humps, on the other hand, are deliberately made.

By you.

You plan them out. (And fight for them with your life.)

A quiet time for prayer each day.

Or Mass during lunch hour.

Perhaps a weekly prayer meeting.

A personal retreat every year.

Humps are special times when you'll ask the very same fundamental questions: *"What's life all about? Where am I going?"* But this time, not because you're forced to, but because you want to.

Take a lot of humps.

Perhaps potholes won't come as often.

---

1 Speedbumps

STOP FOR DIRECTIONS

In my life, I have found three places that give me a deep sense of the presence of God: 1) a scenic mountain with lovely forests; 2) a tranquil beach under a blue sky; 3) and the passenger seat of Roger's red '86 Corolla.

You see, my friend Roger drives like a mad man. Once he starts driving, those riding with him instinctively reach for their wallets and tearfully kiss the photos of their loved ones.

Every time I ride with him, my prayer life is enhanced. Deepened. Invigorated. It feels as though Heaven becomes so near to my soul.

One fateful day, I was riding with him again. We were blazing through a highway like a cruise missile. Roger looked at me and said, *"Bo, I have good news and bad news for you."*

"What's the good news?" I inquired between my Hail Mary's.

"We're efficiently moving at an average speed of 140 kph."

Involuntary spasms shot through my body. *"Are you trying to tell me that we'll be arriving at our destination in no time?"*

"That's the bad news..."

"What?"

"We're lost. I have no idea where we are."
"Stop this car NOW!" I screamed.

We screeched to a halt, asked around, got info, and turned back: we were efficiently and swiftly driving towards the opposite direction. At 140 kph!

I realize that's no isolated incident among human beings. We're prone to commit the same idiocy: we get busy, do a million things, hop here and there, move fast, get efficient.

But gosh, efficiently going where?

What are your highest dreams, anyway?

Your deepest aspirations?

What do you think will give you gut-level, soul-deep joy?

Stop for awhile.

Take a break.

Retreat.

Listen well.

Pray desperately.

Read a map of life.

Know His dreams for you.

When I was thirteen years old, I saw myself doing two things: preaching to a crowd of people and helping the poor. After many years, those two dreams are reality.

I'm a preacher.

And I built ANAWIM, a home for the abandoned elderly and a few orphans.

I've made a decision.

I'm not riding with Roger again until I'm 80.

(No matter how much he assists me with my spiritual life.)

Because I think I still have a few more God–dreams to fulfill.

GOD IS A HAPPY GOD

*L*et me describe to you a hard-headed, stubborn-viewed, narrow-minded, obstinate-thinking, stiff-necked man.

Two guys bump onto each other on the street.

And one says, *"Tom? Wow, Tom! My, you've changed! You were so stout before, and now, you're soooooo thin! And you used to be short, but now you're incredibly tall. And my goodness, you were so fair-skinned before, but you're dark now! And your clothes! You've changed your style! You've changed soooooo much!"*

The other guy says, *"Uh, I'm sorry sir, but I'm not Tom. My name is James."*

"Gosh!" exclaimed the first man, *"You funny boy! You've even changed your name!"*

There are creatures like that in the world today.

About 99.99% of the earth's population, I think.

They'll insist on what they think, perceive, and feel—no matter what reality is screaming at them.

Another example: like I always believed I was ugly. But all the girls around me keep telling me I'm kinda good-lookin'. So what do you think should I do? Be stubborn or open to the truth?

Some may not like that example very much, so I'm giving you another one.

Every time I see a gorgeous sunrise, or play with a

baby, or hear glorious music, or stand on top of a mountain, or run on the beach, or catch a child smile at me—I automatically think that perhaps God must be having fun at that particular moment.

I think: ***God must be a happy God!*** Laughing and having a grand time when He's creating and recreating stuff.

Or why would He make those lovely things?

That's reality. It screams the truth to me!

"Uh, I'm sorry, but I'm not Tom. My name is James."

But you think I'd still believe the truth the next day?

"Gosh, you funny boy! You've even changed your name!"

For when I start my routine of the day, I immediately forget all about my great discovery. In the monotony of my existence, I revert back to my programmed idea of who God is, the image I carried in my brain since I was a scared child spanked by my religion teacher, scolded by a parish priest, and severely warned to be silent in church by my parents: gray throne, long beard, long face, angry eyes.

Suddenly, I'm uneasy with Him. Because He's too serious. If I really want to have fun, I'd do it when He's not watching.

Too bad. 'Coz He wants to have fun with me.

I wonder. *When will I ever get real?*

Please heal my stiff neck, Lord.

YOU CAN CHOOSE
TO BE HAPPY

I recall a few years back, I felt depressed.

I had a million problems! I had conflicts to deal with, a few storms in my Catholic community, plus a number of personal trials as well. To top it all, my dandruff was getting worse and my pimples are erupting again. I prayed, *"Lord, are you sure you want me to continue preaching and writing? I know I'm good-looking* (depression has a way of making me hallucinate)*, but shouldn't You have picked someone much holier and wiser and more loving?"*

As I poured out my grief before God, and as I felt His tender comfort, a crazy question popped in my mind: *"Bo, give me five reasons why you should be happy today."*

"Happy? Lord, how can I be happy at a time like this?"

But the question remained lodged in my brain, and I couldn't give it up.

"Well," I mumbled, *"my five reasons for being happy are lovely Lily, sexy Sylvia, pretty Pamella, terrific Tanya, and gorgeous Grace."* (I was still single at that time, so I could make jokes like these.) Fearing that lighting may strike me anytime, I decided to become serious.

"First reason, Lord: You. We have a great relationship. You love me so much, and uh, I love You sometimes. What a God! Second, I have a beautiful family. Dad's eighty

years old and Mom's (bleep!), yet we're still together… Third, despite of it all, I have a great Catholic group. Fourth, I've got a fantastic job as preacher, writer, helping the poor… Can it be better than this? And fifth, I'm in love with this one girl. (Not five!) *Pretty, sweet, loving, honest, and insane enough to go out on dates with me."*

And before I realized it, my "lousy feelings" left me and I felt happy!

You know, it worked so well, even to this day, I've decided to do this daily. Before I go to bed, I recall five things that happened during that day which I want to be thankful for. It could be small stuff like, *"Today, I watched the sunset;"* or *"A little kid put her arms around me today and that felt so good;"* or *"My wife and I ate at McDonald's 'coz that was all I could afford but felt t'was a candlelight dinner in Shangri-La."*

Because of this practice, the way I see life has changed. Because from the moment I wake up, my antennas are up—looking for the five things I'm going to be thankful for. I'm no longer focused on the bad things that happen, but on God's great blessings each day.

Happiness is a choice.

You and I have everything that we need for happiness. Happiness isn't "out there" but something that's deep within us. We choose to be happy. We choose to make our lives great.

What will you choose?

HAVE FUN WHEN YOU CAN

7:00 AM

One Saturday morning, I kidnap our ANAWIM orphans and kids, all fifteen of them, and squeeze them into my car for a day of fun. Along the way, the kids are singing, dancing, screaming, and vomiting on each other. No wonder my car's air freshener isn't working well. And where are we going? Not to those expensive amusement parks where people pay P400 per head. Multiply that by fifteen, and I'll be poorer than a presidential aspirant who has just lost the elections. Instead, I decide to go to a place that suits my personal tastes and cultural preferences and artistic orientation: a place with no entrance fee.

9:00 AM

I drive them to a free park (Quezon Memorial Circle in Quezon City), rent old bikes—that cost me only P400 for everyone! I spend the whole morning trying to teach the small ones how to balance on a two-wheeler—and wondering whether the big kids left the park and were now biking up Kennon Road to Baguio City.

11:30 AM

As I try to catch my breath, wipe my sweat, and

remove the new designs off my shirt and pants (i.e. bike-tracks), I begin to wonder why I ever got into this thing of putting up an orphanage. Perhaps I should shift careers now. I begin to imagine entering into Showbiz, and making a movie with Cameron Diaz.

12:00 NOON

After failing to catch them with a lasso, or with ingenious pits that I dig and cover with leaves—I give up and softly whisper to myself, *"Kakain na ako. Kung ayaw ninyong kumain, 'di huwag.*[1] Immediately, all fifteen are behind me, little angels in a row.

1:00 PM

After budget meals, plus ice drops—two pesos each—for dessert, I decide on a discovery expedition, to a place that they've never been to. I escort them to a public toilet. Naturally, they are flushed with excitement. After that, it was "swings and slides" time in the park. Life's pleasures are free indeed.

5:00 PM

I'm driving home with my tired crew. I'm exhausted, yes, but peeking through my rear-view mirror, I catch a glimpse of the kids sleeping soundly, and my heart skips a beat.

I love them so much.

One girl was still awake. She sides up to me and whispers, *"Kuya Bo, masayang masaya ako ngayon."*[2] So I wonder if it was the bike ride, or the swing, or the ice drop, or the public toilet. I ask why.

She gives me a tight hug. *"Kasi, kasama ka namin."*[3]

I try to drive carefully. My tears are getting in the way.

---

[1] If you don't want to eat, it's up to you. I'm going to eat now.

[2] Brother Bo, I'm soooo happy.

[3] Because you were with us.

LOVE WITH YOUR HEART

*L*et me speak to married men this time.

One morning, let's say you find your wife in bed with tears in her eyes. When you ask her why, she mumbles, *"I'm depressed."*

As a husband who has read the Bible, attended prayer meetings, and was now active in the parish, the temptation at this point is to love her with your mind. *"What? How could you be depressed?"* You shake your head in dismay. *"Sweetheart, you're not yet spiritually mature! Trust God! Follow Proverbs 3:5 and you won't be depressed! 'Trust in Thy Lord with all thine heart, leaneth not on thine own understanding, in all thy ways acknowledge Him, and He shalt direct thy paths!'"*

If you are the wife, and your husband tells that to you, I'm giving you permission to say to him one of the most expressive words in our language: *"Heh!!!"*

Husbands, don't love her with your mind.

Love her with your heart.

When she says, *"I'm depressed,"* do this: put your arms around her, stroke her hair, and plant a kiss on her forehead. And then say, *"It's okay, hon. It's okay. Can you tell me why you're sad? I'm listening."*

Now imagine your wife says, *"I'm depressed because this morning, I looked at the mirror, and I saw so many wrinkles on my face!"* (Boo-hoo-hoo…)

Immediately, husbands, you'll be tempted to love with your mind again. So you say, *"That's all? Darling, you're vain!"* you say with a preacher's bombastic voice, *"Where's your spiritual maturity? Scripture says, 'Seeketh thy treasure in heaven where thieves doth not break in and steal or moth destroy,' and 'Indeed we believeth that when this earthly tent of ours shall passeth away, we shall findeth a new home, a dwelling in the heavens, not made by human hands, but made by God to last forever!'"*

Husbands, don't love her with your mind.

Love with your heart.[1]

At this point, she doesn't need a preacher. She needs a lover.

Cradle her in your arms again, and if you have a somewhat-tolerable voice, sing to her the love song of Steve Curtis Chapman, *I Will Be Here*. (If your voice chases away cats and dogs, just say the lyrics.)

"I will be here,
You can cry on my shoulder,
When the mirror tells us we're older,
I will hold you,
I will be here,
To watch you grow in beauty…"

---

[1] There is only one time where you should love with your mind, and that's during courtship. Think. Analyze. Evaluate. But once the wedding ceremony is over, the heart rules.

YOU NEVER GRADUATE FROM LOVE'S ACADEMY

Carol was peeking through the window again.

Daily, she'd watch the sweet couple next-door, doing their morning ritual: before the husband went off to work, he'd kiss his wife, give her a hug, and declare to her, *"I love you!"* for all the world to hear. Each morning, Carol saw this sight, and every time, her heart was filled with envy.

Finally, one day, she couldn't take it anymore.

So Carol confronted her husband Pete. "Why can't you be like our next-door neighbor?" She pulled the curtain for him to take a look. "See? This man kisses his wife, embraces her, and says, 'I love you!' every morning. Every morning! Why can't you do that?"

Pete's face was pale. "Honey, I can't do that!"

"Why?" Carol asked angrily.

"Why, Honey, I… I don't even know that woman!"

"Sheeeeeesh. Pete, I'm not asking you to do it with that woman. I'm asking you to do it with me!"

"Oh…" he muttered blankly.

"Tell me that you love me again. I haven't heard it in a long time now!"

Pete shrugged his shoulders. "Gee, Carol, I don't know. I mean, I said, 'I love you' thirty years ago during our honeymoon. And I told you that if I changed my mind, I'd tell you. Well, I haven't."

By now, I think many wives reading this book would like to throw a few cooking pans in the direction of Pete's head.

Let me ask you a question. Why is it necessary for spouses to tell each other, 'I love you' each day? I mean, can't one 'I love you' be sufficient for the next thirty years?

This is the same principle that works for reading the Bible. Or from learning about God. (Huh?)

That's right. As mushy as this may sound, the Bible is God's love letter to you.

And so, in your daily Scripture time, you can't say, *"This is boring. I've read this story before;"* or, *"Oh no, today's reading is the Prodigal Son again. Gosh, I've read this a million times;"* or, *"The beatitudes? Again? I can recite that in my sleep!"*

So what? You see, you're forgetting one thing: Christianity isn't just a religion. It's primarily a *relationship.*

It's a personal relationship where 'I love you' is repeated for a million times.

The temptation among Christians is to look for the new, the esoteric, the higher learning, the advanced subjects with big words—thinking that they can graduate from the basics. Stuff like trust. Obedience. Humility. Faith. Surrender. And God whispering, 'I love you' in our hearts again and again and again.

If you feel like you can graduate from the basic stuff, I think you're in the wrong religion. Because this one has no graduates.

We remain students of love, forever.

STOP COMPARING
AND START LIVING

*R*emember when we were kids?

One little tyke will say, "My grandfather's house is so large, it has forty-two rooms!"

"Wala 'yan sa bahay ng Lolo ko!"[1] his playmate chimes up, "To go from the kitchen to the living room, you have to ride a tricycle."

Naturally, the third boy speaks up, not wanting to be beaten. *"Hah! Wala 'yan sa bahay ng Lolo ko!* If you're in the dining room, and you want to call the people to eat, you'll have to phone them in their bedrooms—and you'll have to pay long-distance charges!"

Kids do that sort of thing. And we laugh.

But when adults do the same thing—it's utterly embarrassing!

But then of course, what should we expect? Where did the kids learn it from, anyway? (I'm gonna bet we learned some of it from our mothers.)

I remember the story of the four mothers who were nursing their babies, chatting over a cup of tea. One of them said, "My son will be famous when he grows up. He'll be a Bishop, and when people see him, they'll say, 'Your Excellency…'"

"Peanuts," groaned the other mom. "That's nothing. When my son grows up, he'll be a Cardinal, and when people see him, they'll say, 'Your Eminence…'"

"Tsk, tsk, tsk. Too bad," piped up the other woman, "because my son will be Pope, and when people see him, they'll say, 'Your Holiness…'"

The fourth mother was silent, patting her little bundle of joy. So the other women were intrigued and asked her, "And what will your son be when he grows up, hmm?"

She smiled. "Oh, he'll just be a priest."

"Just a priest?" the others asked incredulously.

"Yes. And he'll only be a short fellow, maybe 5 feet tall. But he'll weigh a horrendous 350 pounds. So that when people see him, they'll say, 'Oh my God…'"

I remember I came from our prayer meeting, and my friend Mike Joseph Jr. preached to us that day. Mike's a terrific preacher, and so I told my mother that I really loved his preaching. Mom answered, "Yeah, I liked his preaching, too. But Bo, face it—no one can preach as good as you do."

Wow. The President and Founder of Bo's International Fan's Club, in action!

I guess we've got this crazy thing in us that wants to know "who's better," "who's bigger," "who's richer," "who's more beautiful"—and even "who's holier!"

But I believe this is the source of much discontent in our lives.

Really!

If we can only stop comparing ourselves with others, I

believe that we'll be happier and more at peace within.
    My suggestion? Be yourself.
    Live your life.
    Do the best you can, and leave the rest to God.
    And you'll be at peace.
    (And finally, our *Lolo*s can rest in peace as well.)

---

[1] That's nothing compared to my grandfather's house!

BELIEVE IN YOURSELF THE WAY GOD BELIEVES IN YOU

*Y*esterday, I met her again after a long, long time. Aida.

A mother of six children, loving wife, and pure *Ilocana*.[1]

A leader of a small prayer group.

Perhaps twenty or thirty people.

I visited her again, and was struck at how so many things have *not* changed. I went to the living room where I used to sit as a thirteen-year-old boy. The plastic leatherette chair felt small now. But the old brown piano was still there—and at once, I could hear the old charismatic songs of years gone by. *This Is The Day* and *Oh, What A Mighty God We Serve* and *Come, Holy Spirit, I Need You*. Funny how everything started to come back.

I remember how I had a big crush on Aida's eldest daughter. She played the piano so gloriously, I wanted to do the same. Well yesterday, I met her there—already a doctor, married, and with a wonderful baby.

Everything was coming back.

The walls. The picture frames. The windows with old-fashioned curtains.

The past started coming alive.

"You shall preach next Friday, Bo"

It was as though I could hear Aida's voice.

A motherly voice that was gentle yet strong.

More than any other, these were the "sacred" words that changed the direction of my life. The thirteen-year-old boy looked up and nodded.

"Okay," I said meekly to her.

I didn't know what else to say. But at the back of my mind, I wondered, "Why me?" I was the youngest in the group.

So the following week, I preached my first talk.

It was a disaster.

But Aida's belief in me was unflinching. She smiled all through my talk. And right after the "disaster," she told me to give another "disaster" the following Friday.

That was more than two decades ago.

Today, I'm a preacher. And I love my job. I have reached millions of people with God's Word, all over the world.

Why?

Because of one woman who believed in me.

One woman who to this day leads a small group of twenty people.

As I say this, I already imagine Aida shaking her head. She will tell me with a smile, "Well, how could I not believe in you? *God* believed in you, Bo."

As I look back, I sometimes have tears in my eyes—thinking what would I be now without an Aida in my life.

May you find one in your journey. (We need a

handful of them around us.)

People who believe in you so much, they'll be willing to accept the early disasters that will flow out of our budding greatness.

– 0 –

I've got another idea.

Be an *Aida* for someone else.

There is always one person out there that you know who will bless so many others—if only someone will believe in them, the way God believes in them.

Will you?

God believes you can.

---

[1] A person from Ilocos, a Northern province of the Philippines

MAKE ENJOYING LIFE
A MASTER SKILL

I'm in Tagaytay [1] now and life is glorious up here.

I was able to borrow from a friend her pretty house that sits right on the ridge—with a porch overlooking the breathtaking Taal lake and Taal Volcano.

It's early morning, and the view is majestic. I breathe this all in as I sit on a nice wooden chair, in front of a tiny table—where my coffee cup rests. Not a styropor or plastic cup, mind you. But china. So that it makes nice "tinkling" sounds when you swirl your teaspoon around.

Actually, I'm not a coffee drinker.

But the entire scene "demanded" that I drink one.

While I do this, I read a good, fat book.

Ahhh.

Why is life soooooo good?

Life *is* beautiful.

If there's one thing that defines me, it's this line: *I know how to get a kick out of life.* Enjoying life is my master skill. I'm able to squeeze every drop of joy and blessing from the simplest, most ordinary experiences of each day. (Even the most painful ones! But that's another chapter...)

Actually, I don't need the Taal lake to make me happy.

I don't need the wooden chair or the tiny table or the coffee cup.

I don't need the good, fat book.

I just need to be me—and I'm happy with me! I actually like *my* company!

Some people are very "iffy" about their happiness. "*If* I get a new job, then I'll be happy," or "*If* I get married, then I'll be happy," or "*If* I get a car, then I'll be happy," or "*If* I buy a house, then I'll be happy."

They've got one rude awakening coming up real soon.

Because the truth is, **if they're not happy now, where they are, they won't be happy no matter what happens to them.**

Some people create elaborate, complicated, sometimes *impossible* rules to experience happiness in their lives. Like, "*Unless everyone loves me and accepts me, I'll never be happy.*" Pretty insane, right?

Some have other types of complicated rules to gaining happiness: "*I will be happy only if I'll be able to buy a BMW, wear an Armani, a Rolex watch…*" Poor creatures!

Others are such demanding lovers that they're doomed to always be unhappy in their relationships. They say, "I'll be happy only if my beloved will wait on me 24 hours a day, think of me always, serve me attentively, and eat, walk, talk, breathe for me!"

God have mercy on their loved ones.

My conditions to experiencing happiness are pretty simple:

If I breathe normally, I'll be happy.

If I feel my heart pumping in my chest, I'll be happy.

If the sun shines today, I'll be happy—even if the sun shines behind storm clouds!

If I'm able to smile, I'll be happy.

If I'll be able to love someone in whatever small way, I'll be happy.

And most of all, if God loves me, I'll really be happy. (When doesn't He?)

Haven't you noticed? *I cheat on life.* Because I make my own rules to experiencing happiness, and I make them so simple, they're stacked on my favor.

I have a suggestion for you. Examine your conditions for happiness now.

They may be too darn complicated, you'll never be happy in your life.

Too bad.

Because life is too beautiful to miss out.

---

[1] A favorite tourist spot famous for its cool temperature and scenic views.

NURTURE YOUR SECRET LIFE

"*Your assignment is to clean the toilet everyday.*"

Many years ago, I was part of a celibate brotherhood. And on my first day there, an older brother gave me my assigned chore: Toilet cleaning.

"I don't know how to clean toilets," I muttered meekly, "can you teach me?"

"Let's start with the toilet bowl," he smiled, as he grabbed a sponge, sank his hand into the toilet water, and started scrubbing the insides of the bowl. Believe me, every hair on my body stood on end and my innards shook violently.

"Gee… uh, I recall Mom using a stick…" I mumbled, but he interrupted, "But this cleans it so much better," his forearm almost disappearing inside the Throne.

With his hand still dripping, he handed me the sponge and said, "You want to try?" I almost choked and wondered if God could take my life that second.

"Okay…" I held the foam as manly as I could. Being at a loss for words, I started praying in tongues. I plunged my hand into the water, and realized that my state-of-life discernment was over. That very night, I was going to escape the brotherhood, and get married.

But the days became weeks, and the weeks, months.

I cleaned that toilet for a whole year. And I began to love it. It became "*my* toilet" and "*my* sponge." I'd have withdrawal pangs if I didn't clean the toilet in a day.

Indeed, the celibate brotherhood taught me the meaning of *The Secret Life*.

You see, I was already preaching in big prayer rallies at that time. After such events, people took my pictures, got my autograph, and—hear this—tried very hard to shake my hand. Oh, if they only knew what I held just a few hours before.

My "public life" was symbolized by the microphone.

But my "secret life" was symbolized by the sponge. And it put me in my place, keeping pride away from my heart.

I love Bill Hybell's definition of "Character:" ***Character is who you are when no one's looking.*** It's easy to be a disciple in front of an applauding crowd. But when no one's looking, was I still a disciple?

Thanks to my sponge, I had an answer: Yes!

I remember one Saturday night. We had a big feast—and all the brothers washed the dishes together. We even sang happy songs while soaping, rinsing, and drying.

That night, I was soaping. When it was almost over, I was removing a stubborn food particle stuck in a fork—when I noticed something about the sponge in my hand. It looked oddly familiar.

I gasped. Because I knew *my* sponge! What was it doing here in the kitchen? Just to be sure, I rushed to the toilet and opened the cabinet under the sink—the usual place where I stored my sponge. It wasn't there.

I entered the kitchen hesitantly, wondering whether to tell the brothers or not. But I saw them singing and happy. How could I break their cheery mood? So I decided to join the singing, get *my* sponge, and soap the few remaining plates. (To this day, I have never told them what had happened that night. When they read this article, they will kill me.)

I have a question for you: How's your secret life?

Who are you when no one's looking?

In the unspectacular, mundane, routine of your day?

I tell you. Nurture your secret life.

$-0-$

I believe that on Judgement Day, God will give me a 365-room mansion in heaven. And when I ask Him why the lavish reward, I'd expect Him to say, *"Because of your preaching to thousands,"* or *"Because you founded a Home for the Elderly,"* etc. But instead, He'd say, *"For each day you cleaned that toilet with love in your heart..."*

LIFE IS GOOD IF YOU LOVE

*T*here are some things in life that I deeply enjoy.

Like standing on top of a serene mountain breathing in God's beauty.

Or simply reading a delicious book that I can't put down.

Or just being hugged by a little child.

Or eating ice cream with friends.

But there is this one specific thing that I do which I find exquisitely sweet. Awesome even. It's probably one of the most profoundly inspiring things that I do.

You might think it's preaching. Or writing. Or leading worship.

Believe me, I love doing those things.

But I'm thinking of something else.

(Something downright simple.)

I'm talking about cutting Dad's fingernails.

And toenails.

You see, Dad is eighty years old—and he can't see very well anymore.

So whenever I'm at home, this elderly man lumbers towards me, and very shyly, shows me his fingernails and toenails. He doesn't have to say anything. He just chuckles. And I understand.

So I get my heavy-duty, industrial-strength, kryptonite nailclipper. And we go to work. I also wear bullet-proof goggles to protect my eyes, lest they be injured by flying shrapnel. Beside me is a chain-saw, just in case my nail-clipper won't do.

But as I do this, my heart melts within.

Because many years ago, I still remember when he'd do this for me. As a little boy, I'd sit on his lap, and he'd hold my tiny hands and with great care cut my nails. I remember him doing this again and again and again…

Those were also the days when he'd bring me to the barber shop. As I'd sit on the high chair, he'd tell the barber what to do. "Make him *guwapo*[1]," he'd command.

Today, things are little bit different. I now bring him to the barber—after some shy signals from him that he doesn't want to look like Freddie Aguilar.[2] With a sheepish smile, he'd form his fingers like scissors and run them through his grayish hair. And so I'd drive him to a near-by barber shop, trying to stop my tears from falling. And when he'd plop on the chair, I'd tell the barber what to do. "Make him *guwapo* like me," I'd command.

Life is good.

Why?

Because life gives me precious moments to say "thanks" to special people.

Because life gives me abundant opportunities to genuinely love.

Because life gives me a way to be a better person, everyday.

---

[1] good-looking
[2] A famous Filipino male folksinger with shoulder-length hair.

IN EVERY TRIAL,
THERE IS A TREASURE

I now realize that joy or misery is a choice that we have to make daily.

This came to me strongly when one day, I was driving in Novaliches with my family to visit some relatives. Because of the enormous roadwork there, we got lost taking alternative routes. Besides, Novaliches is famous for an amazingly circuitous network of streets—reminding me of my intestines.

"Can you help us find this address?" my Mom asked a guy driving a little jeep. "Sure," he said, "follow me. I'm going in that direction…"

And we did: for about two hours! He led us through the inner labyrinths of Novaliches. Through dark alleys. Through pot holes. Through dirt roads. In total, we took 32 rights, 47 lefts, and 13 U-turns.

All the while, my family was complaining like crazy. "We're lost!" they whined. "Oh, why all these roadwork at the same time?" another grumbled. "And who's this guy leading us anyway? We don't know him at all! He could be…" And there was a tense-filled pause. Finally, one family member said, "Oh my God. We're being kidnapped! WE'RE BEING KIDNAPPED BY THAT MAN!" (Divulging identities of who said what has proven hazardous to my health, so I'll refrain from mentioning names here.)

I had to laugh and say, "C'mon, the guy doesn't look like a kidnapper at all…"

"Really? Good…" sighed everyone.

"He's no kidnapper," I shook my head, "I think he's a serial killer."

Boy, were they mad and miserable.

What was I doing all this time?

Aside from driving for them, I was also singing. I was having the time of my life. I was excited making those zigs and zags! Under my breath, I prayed, *"Lord, I thank You that I feel like Indiana Jones trapped in a maze. What a thrilling adventure!"*

Generally, I was thanking God for blessing us. I was thanking God for those rare times that I'm with my family—no matter how crazy they may be. I was thanking God for my car. I was thanking God for the relatives we were visiting. I was thanking God for sending us an angel as our guide—using a serial killer to lead our way. Because I was so busy being grateful, I realized I didn't have time to be miserable!

When we finally reached the home of our relatives, my family stepped down from the car with angry exasperation. And that was when the real performance began. (All the complaining they did in the car was just dress rehearsal.) *"We had a terrrrrrrrible time!"* they griped in unison as they greeted our cousins. As they were replaying their sad ordeal to them, I opened the car door, stepped down, stretched my tired muscles, and smiled, *"Ahhh… Now was that exciting or what?"*

One week after, every time my family got together, they'd still grumble and relive the agony of that trip. (At some special days, the *Nightmare in Novaliches* had matinee shows in the afternoons and main performances in the evenings.)

But I recall the event with sweetness. And fun!

Because every morning, I face the mirror and tell myself, "Bo, no one can take away your joy. This is the day that the Lord has made, let us rejoice and be glad in it!"

Because I believe that *in every problem, there's a rich blessing.*

In every trial, there's a treasure waiting to be unearthed.

YOUR PRIMARY GIFTS WILL LEAD YOU TO YOUR SACRED MISSION

I've always been a communicator ever since I can remember.

As a small kid, I used to have a collection of humor books. Like I remember ripping out the pages of *Laughter, the Best Medicine* of all the issues of *Reader's Digest*, and compiling them into a single fat book. I'd memorize these jokes and retell them to my family. (There came a time when I told and retold my jokes so often that everyone memorized them as well. So in order to save time, we just assigned each of these jokes a number. For example, I'd scream, *"Joke #28!"* and everyone would break out laughing.)

And as a ten-year-old boy, I drew my own comic books. Superman, Batman, Wonder Woman, and a slew of Japanese robots came to life at the back pages of my Science, Social Studies, and Math notebooks. Until I made my own super-hero (me), saving the world from vicious aliens (my sisters).

Some time later, as an early teen, I tried writing my own fiction novel. I only reached chapter two, and everyone who read it didn't understand a thing I wrote—but hey, at least I could claim I was a budding novelist.

But at age thirteen, I gave my first talk in a small prayer meeting—and I've not stopped preaching since.

At fourteen, I began writing worship songs.

Years later, I found myself publishing magazines, writing books, preaching through radio, TV, and teaching tapes. And having enormous fun!

Deep within, I realized that God has made me His communicator.

Because I love proclaiming truth in a simple, understandable way.

I love telling stories that inspire, that give life, that empower.

I love the feel of an old Bible in my hand, as I sit in front of my desk or squat under a tree—praying, thinking, and creating a talk that'll give hope to those who'll hear.

I also love the sight of an empty computer screen. I feel a rush of excitement in my veins the moment my fingers touch the keyboard, poised for action, ready to give birth to an article that will bless many.

That's how God made me.

And I need to be true to my primary gift—for there lies my *sacred mission.*

I don't know what your first gift is, but you'll find in it the *handwriting* of God. It'll point you to your life-project, your assigned-purpose, your God-ordained mission.

By the way, it will also point you to your happiness.

Recently, I've unloaded most of my "noncommunicating" work. Like managing organizations and communities, and holding endless meetings and planning sessions! I was doing stuff like that for years, because we were pioneering. But after praying and searching hard, God has raised up others—those whose primary gift *is* management. I realize now that I thwart God's over-all plan if I insist on taking work that isn't my primary gift. *Because the enemy of the best is the second best.*

I've made a decision. I'm focusing on what I do best.

Let me ask you now: **What is your primary gift?** Live it to the max.

FRIENDSHIPS ARE YOUR GREATEST TREASURE

When I was single, I did everything with lightning speed.

I remember it took me only nine minutes to eat breakfast, shower, dress up, and get ready to drive off to wherever. No kidding.

When I got married, preparing to leave home takes me a little bit more time. (About one hour and fifty-one minutes more.)

Don't get me wrong. I'm not complaining.

You see, my wife is a woman.

(Thank God.)

If I wanted to continue my quick pace in life, I should have remained single. Or married another guy. Which would look strange, especially that I'm a preacher.

You see, I'm the typical male that's totally goal-fixated. Men are creatures of *purpose* while women are creatures of *process*.

Let me explain it another way: As a man, I don't care much for the journey—just the destination. So the shorter the trip, the better. My wife, however, loves every inch of the journey. She walks leisurely, hums a tune, pauses for scenery.

That's why each morning, she enjoys a cool shower, while I just try to get moist. And that's why she treats as near-sacred her time in front of an open closet, choosing and re-choosing what clothes to wear. I, however, just grab what I wore yesterday.

But more importantly, this is the reason why my wife majors in *relationships*, and I don't think much about them. Because relationships don't have purposes; the relationship *is* the purpose.

Like if I sprint out of the house while stuffing breakfast in my mouth, my wife takes delight in a slow meal, where food isn't the only thing shared, but conversation, stories, warmth, and laughter.

She also has the time to regularly stop her work to check on the state of our friendship. She asks, *"Do you love me?"* When I respond, *"Yes, I do,"* she teases, *"How much?"* After I tell her, *"Very much,"* she peacefully goes back to whatever she was doing. This dialogue is repeated about fourteen times in a regular day.

Because of her, I've learned anew an ancient truth: *That friendships are the most sacred, most precious, most life-giving stuff of human life.*

They are our richest treasure!

My friends are many.

God is my first Friend.

I consider my wife to be my best friend.

And I have my family and my community as wonderful, beautiful friends.

As I waste my time with them and wonder whether I'm accomplishing anything, I have to hammer this reality to my head: Friendships are not about goals or purposes or results. Because friendship, in essence, is the journey *and* the destination.

I've now learned that relationships are more important than accomplishments.

That time-efficiency is second only to love-efficiency.

That nurturing friendship is the greatest thing that I can ever accomplish in life.

In essence, that's my purpose for being.

(Male thinking, hmm?)

ONLY GOD IS NOT A SEASON

*F*ive years ago, I decided to live without a salary.

Just because I felt... well, I felt God wanted me to do it.

I didn't care if people called me cookoo, or screwball, or ding-a-ling. But I wanted to try living in trust, waiting on Heaven for my next meal, my next ride, my next hair-cut. Even just for a season. So I told my organizations NOT to give me a paycheck.

So there were days when I, Chairman of the Board, went past a McDonald's hungry, because my pockets were empty. There were days when I walked home because I didn't have enough fare. There were weeks when I was tempted to don a ponytail because I couldn't afford a haircut. (I recall that this ponytail-ordeal came to an abrupt end when I received ten thousand bucks from a total stranger. I quickly ran to the barbershop and asked for the most expensive hair-cut they had, telling them, *"You can dye my hair purple!"*)

My season of comfortable poverty lasted for almost three years.

But ironically, in those same years, I also traveled to three cities in the U.S., five cities in Canada, one city in Africa, four cities in Europe, two trips to Israel, and four cities in Asia. All for free, because I was invited to preach and to guide people in pilgrimages. (I remember leaving for my foreign trips with a nice coat and tie, so no one would think I only had twenty dollars in my wallet.)

But like the way it began, I felt a surging inspiration within me that my season of happy poverty was to end. So three years after, I allowed my organizations to pay me a salary again. (Would you believe? I have a savings account now—something I had to look into the dictionary to find out what the word meant.)

I have no regrets entering into that season.

Because I believe I've learned one great lesson of life: *That seasons of famine are permitted by God to give us deepened trust.*

If we have everything—and everything goes on smoothly in our lives—we will never know what it means to really, really, reeeeeeeeally trust.

It's easy to say, "*I trust God*" when you're vacationing in a Luxury Love Boat, dining in one of it's classy restaurants, napkin on your chest, munching on shark meat dipped in *wasabe* and soy sauce. But it's not so easy to say, "*I trust God*" when your Love Boat has just capsized, and you're now in the open sea, surrounded by giant sharks with napkins on their chests, bringing with them their own *wasabe* and soy sauce.

But that's the point! There's really no difference between those two scenes! You need to trust God fully, whatever the season you're in!

Two Questions.

Are you going through a season of abundance?
Being paid a nice salary, huh? Don't trust it.
Employed by a large multi-national company? I don't care how secure you think it is, I'm telling you: it's not.

In the end, you know who will never fail.

Or are you going through a season of poverty or hardship or trial?
Believe me. That will end.
Because they are simply that: seasons.
Only God is not a season.
Only He will never end.

THE FASTEST GUY DOESN'T WIN THE RACE

"*B*o, you're a workaholic!"

Every time I heard that line, I swelled with pride within, hid it beneath a shy smile, and muttered, "*Aw shucks, maybe just a little. But thank you anyway…*"

I loved being a workaholic! And I loved it when others told me I was one!

At a time when the word "multi-tasking" wasn't invented yet, I was already an avid practitioner. I was head of several Catholic communities (I lost count somewhere along the way), chairman of an aggressive Catholic publications firm, and director of a new ministry for the poor. Add to that my passion as a writer and preacher—traveling here and abroad—and you'll get an idea of the kind of insane lifestyle I lived.

But I was proud of that busy, albeit harassed, schedule.

I didn't (and couldn't) walk or drive from meeting to meeting. I had to rush, and zoom, and dash, and whisk, and jet, and zip, and race, and torpedo my way!

In other words, I didn't have time to live.

Well one day, I just realized I was doing it all wrong.

Because no matter how hard or how fast I worked, I didn't feel I was going anywhere. My relationships weren't growing. I felt I wasn't genuinely loving people anymore. Nor was I enjoying life. Even God seemed far away.

I woke up and realized that *workaholism* was a disease. (For me, it was an addiction of trying to win the love of people. I was running away from who I was, which deep within, I didn't like very much.)

So finally, one glorious day, I made a crucial choice.

I decided to semi-retire.

And I decided to really live.

Because I realized I got the rules all wrong.

The fastest guy didn't win the race.

But the guy who had the most love—and joy and peace—when he got to the finish line.

Winners were those who had the relaxed time of smelling beautiful flowers along the way. Winners had the ability to stop whatever they were doing to encourage other wounded runners. And winners had the power to sing most of the way.

One day, I simply gave up 80% of my responsibilities to friends who could do a better job. (When you think that I was doing the work of five men, giving up that 80% only meant that I'm finally doing what one man should be doing!)

Now, I have time to smell the flowers.

To taste my food.

To breathe fresh air.

To enjoy majestic scenery.

To listen to the music of the wind.

To gaze at my wife and see how lovely she is.

To laugh with old friends and thank God for each of them.

And to love.

(To really, really, really love.)

WIPE WHILE WET

"*L*et's have our apartment repainted!" my happy wife announced one day.

"Great idea!" I nodded with glee, "and you know what? I'll do it myself!"

Suddenly, her demeanor changed. Even her skin color grew pale. She was speechless, her jaw agape. (The last time I saw that "God-help-me" look on her face was when I first proposed to her.) "Umm, on second thought," she muttered weakly, "I think our home looks just fine. The old paint in fact adds character and charm…"

But it was useless. I already was off to the hardware. And I knew what my wife was thinking: That I have never painted a house before. But didn't she know that I painted a lot of other stuff? So when I arrived with twenty-five gallons of paint in my car trunk, I tried to cheer her up. "Honey, don't worry. I 'water colored' in kindergarten. In fact, my teacher displayed two of my art works on her bulletin board!"

Well today, our tiny abode is newly painted. But so is everything else in it, under it, above it, around it—including the mailman that came at the wrong time when I was putting a twenty-sixth coat on the front door. Even my teeth had paint on them. The only part of my body that didn't have paint on was my intestines.

In other words, being totally ignorant about painting, I dripped, spilled, smudged, smeared, splashed paint on every dead or living object found within a two-mile radius around our apartment. (I literally painted the town red. And white, blue, brown…)

But you know what? My clumsiness was saved by one of the greatest contraptions ever invented by humankind: *A wet rag*. No kidding.

Whenever my brush dripped, slipped, or painted something that shouldn't have been painted, all I had to do was wipe it off with a moist cloth—and eureka! it was gone.

But here's the rule: *Wipe while wet*. I mean, don't let a minute pass by. Never, ever let it dry. Because if it does, God have mercy on you. Like it took me two weeks to scrape, rub, and peel the dried-up paint around the house. I used thinner, detergent, cleanser, muriatic acid, sulphuric acid, even ascorbic acid. I even sprinkled holy water.

May I have your full attention please?

This isn't a lecture on painting houses. This is a reflection on the *life of a soul*.

You see, we make mistakes quite often. We spill, smear, splash our souls dirty. All of us do. We think foul thoughts. Dirty thoughts. Vengeful thoughts. Evil thoughts.

But here's the catch. With one stroke, we can remove them easy—as long as they're still wet. Trust me, they don't stand a chance. As long we don't take too long, we can get rid of evil from our minds—and lives.

Oh yes, they do return. Again, and again, and again. They're pretty stubborn, these fellows. But with one stroke, we can wipe them off. Again, and again, and again.

The point: **Be as stubborn as they are.** If we don't, we're going to scrubbing dried-up sin in our souls for days, perhaps months, possibly years—even a lifetime. Because our thoughts become our deeds, our deeds become our character, our character become our destiny.

Because of this, I now know what hell may look like: *It's a place where the soul is violently, fiercely scrubbing off evil from every square inch of its skin—till it's one grotesque body of festering wounds—but he'll just keep on scratching and rubbing and scraping for all his painful eternity.*

My friend, carve this on stone: Wipe while wet.
It might just save you an eternity.

ONLY LOVE HEALS

Yesterday, I read about this woman who bought a parrot from a pet store. But she went back the next day complaining to the sales lady, "It hasn't spoken a single word!" So the sales clerk advised, "Why don't you buy a mirror? Some parrots need to see themselves to get them talking." Excitedly, the woman bought a mirror and went home.

The next day, she came back and said, "It ain't talking yet!" The sales clerk suggested a ladder this time. "Moving up and down the ladder may stimulate the parrot to speak." So she purchased a tiny ladder for the parrot.

But the next day, she came barging back into the store declaring, "Nothing has worked! It hasn't made a sound." The sales clerk was equally frustrated and said, "How about a nice seesaw? That sometimes helps them get more verbally active." So off the woman went with her seesaw.

Finally, the next morning, the woman returns forlorn. "It's dead," she groaned.

"Oh no!" The sales lady inquired, "Did it even say one word before it died?"

"Well, yes," the woman sighed, "before it dropped dead, it said, 'Doesn't that pet store sell any food?'"

I've been part of Catholic communities most of my

life, and one of the humbling realizations I have had is that as members, we can get very enamored and impressed with the mirrors, the ladders, and seesaws of community life. We're green with envy when we hear that other "bigger" communities have "more" to offer—more teachings, more ministries, more programs. So we get very busy to be like them, creating sophisticated teaching programs, detailed organization charts, with complex outreach ministries. And yet at the end of the day, do we starve ourselves dry?

We can get so preoccupied with other stuff, *we don't have time to love people.*

Because we can have the best preachers, the best evangelists, the best teachers—but **if our leaders are not first of all** *lovers*, **community life will not last.** (The forms, activities, and structures may remain, but if you look inside, it's hollow. People are dying because they're not receiving love—or giving it to each other.)

That's pathetic.

The more I live in community, the more I believe that it's essentially about "loving friends." That's as corny, as simple, as glorious as I can define it. Bottom line, community is about loving each other in ordinary, nondramatic, unspectacular ways.

A phone call when someone is sick.

A simple meal together with lots of laughter.

A small note for a discouraged companion.

A prayer intention.

A warm hug for an older member of community.

A small cash gift when a friend is out of job.

An offer to baby-sit for a tired mother.

(In the end, these are the simple things that will make us saints!)

As a leader, I know I can't personally love every single member of my community—for they number in the thousands. But if I can try to love—and be a real friend—to those closest to me, then perhaps that love will be passed on.

Because only love heals.

Only love nourishes.

Only love makes community.

HARD WORK MAGIC *WORKS*

I smiled at the lovely woman beside me.

She smiled back, her large round eyes singing.

Hard as I tried, I couldn't recall gazing at a more ravishing sight in my life. And it wasn't just physical, mind you. It was her peaceful presence, her gentle nature, her bearing both feminine and strong at the same time.

"Good day, isn't it?" I intoned, attempting to hide my nervousness.

"Yes, though it's a teensy bit warm," her soft voice whispered.

In truth, the day was hot and the air quite still. But I was oblivious to it, caught up in the vision of the angel before me, as though the very air I breathed was part of this apparition of loveliness.

"Are you… uh, doing anything tonight?"

The princess chuckled. "Why do you ask?"

"Well, I was wondering if you'd like to spend it with me. Alone, if possible." My voice trembled and my chest felt like it wanted to explode.

"Aren't you going a little too fast?"

Her naughty grin gave me confidence, so I shook my head. "Nope. In fact, I think the timing is more than perfect."

She squinted. "We'll see. If you do the right

things and say the right words..."

Suddenly, the Bishop—who was in front of us—announced, *"Dearly beloved, this is the wedding of the century!"* At once, a thousand people cheered behind us. Marowe, radiant in her white wedding gown, gave out a shy giggle. I laughed more uproariously.

His excellency asked us a number of questions.

I recall answering, *"Yes, I do,"* to each of them. He told me to put a ring on her finger, and I followed the instructions to the letter. I guess I did the right things and said the right words that day, because my bride obliged my request. We did spend the rest of the day together. And the next 365 days thereafter.

Yes, it's been a year since, and I've learned some truths about being a lover.

One is that all apparitions of loveliness, no matter how lovely, will not last. After awhile, every enchanting princess becomes a broom-riding witch. (And I, the gorgeous prince in her eyes, turns into an insect-munching, slimy-skinned, foul-smelling toad.) This happens to everybody. No exceptions.

But here's the second truth I've learned: That this too isn't a permanent condition.

That if I keep on **doing the right things** and **saying the right words** each day—I can bring back our romance to life again. *If I continue to say "Yes" to God's questions of love, and follow His instructions to the letter... the apparition of loveliness in my heart returns*. No doubt about it.

With a kiss, the frog becomes a prince again—and

the witch a lovely princess once more. Yes, it is magic, but magic that you work very hard for.

To my forever bride, thank you for a magical first year. The many times we laughed. The many times we cried. Even the many times we fought—and ended up in each others' arms before the end of each day. Yes, you are the most beautiful gift God has ever given me. Next to God, you will always be the greatest thing that ever happened to me.

GOD ANSWERS PRAYER
HIS WAY

When my wife announced to me that she was pregnant, we embraced each other for the longest time I can remember. We acted like lunatics. We sang. We danced. We cried. So this was how it felt.

I was going to be a father. This can't be real, I told myself. But it was true! Spontaneously, I straightened my back, expanded my chest, and beamed a brand-new-Daddy's smile.

So each day, we prayed for our little miracle, laying our hands on her tummy. Every night, I spoke to our child, whispering gently, "Baby, do you know that I love you very much? Mommy loves you a lot, too. And God loves you even more." Each night, I'd say these lines over and over again. And each night, I'd read aloud the Gospel of the day, and added my own homily. Stuff like, "You see, baby, the Greek word *Logos* in John 1:1 is epistemologically rooted in a very rich hermeneutic context..."

I imagined my little baby nodding her head. I also wondered if she'd become a preacher one day. Or perhaps a writer. But it didn't matter, really. Because my daily prayer was, *"Lord, make her a happy child, and she can be anything You want her to be!"*

God took that prayer seriously and answered it one day after Christmas.

We were spending the holidays with the poor, the elderly, and the orphans in ANAWIM. That afternoon, my wife saw a small drop of dried blood on her undergarments. Was this something to worry about? We didn't think so.

We were wrong.

Two days later, at 6:00 AM, I found my wife sobbing and shaking uncontrollably in the bathroom. She pointed to the mass of blood in the toilet bowl, and I quickly grabbed my trembling wife and held her in my arms.

We lost our baby.

"Angel shall be your name," I managed to say, my voice failing me, "and I baptize you in the name of the Father, and of the Son, and of the Holy Spirit."

Yes, Baby Angel is your name.

Not once did we feel what it was like to cradle you in our arms.

Not once did we feel the thrill of watching you make your first tiny steps.

Not once did we feel the inner pleasure of hearing you say, "Mommy" and "Daddy."

But you see, that doesn't change the fact that you are our child.

And Angel is your name.

God did answer our prayer. You are a happy child today, far more than we can ever imagine. And He made you what He wanted you to be.

For God so determined that it is you Angel who now cradles us in your arms of prayer. And it's you, Angel, who thrills in watching our every step, our every move, our every breath. And it's you who have not stopped saying "Mommy" or "Daddy" since you entered the portals of Heaven, for you mention our names before God everyday.

You were never with us, **and yet will always be with us.**

And no one can take you away from us anymore.
For Angel is your name.

BE A DOLPHIN, NOT A SHARK

A guy with a large black Bible clutched under his arm rode the jeepney I was on. At once, I noticed that peculiar glazed look on his eye and the friendly smile on his face—and I knew it wouldn't be too long before he'd make his first move. In my next breath, bingo, he cornered his first victim—a college girl beside him— with the question asked in a typical preacher's modulated voice, *"Friend, are you saved?"*

Instantly, the young woman nervously faced the other way.

Undeterred, the zealous evangelist turned next to the fiftyish man in front of the woman and inquired, *"Do you know Jesus Christ?"*

You won't believe what this man did: He signaled the driver to stop and got off immediately. But I shivered when I realized I was the only passenger in the jeepney left to talk to. We smiled at each other, and I wondered what his opening line would be.

"Friend, if you die right now," he asked with utter seriousness, *"do you know where you would go?"*

My eyes squinted. *"Um, let me see… Funeraria Paz? Eternal Gardens?"*

My evangelist's jaw fell to the floor.

I chuckled and held out my hand to him, *"I'm Bo. I'm also a Christian."*

He laughed and asked, *"What church do you attend, brother?"*

"The Catholic Church," I said as matter-of-factly as I could.

"Oh… that," he muttered, swallowing hard. His face likened that of one whose mother had just passed away. *"Then, you are* not *a Christian,"* he said somberly, *"for I too was a former Catholic until God saved me from that Babylonian religion."*

At that point, I regretted why I ever began the conversation. I've been in these situations before where I defended my Catholic faith, but always I felt I was talking to a brick wall. So I decided to do what one does to brick walls.

I avoid them. *"I'll see you in Heaven!"* I told him, as I stepped down the jeepney.

As I watched the vehicle roar away, the evangelist was now talking to the driver.

Now don't get me wrong. I admire guys like him. Their zeal, their sincerity, their courage to talk to total strangers. But it's the same type of admiration that one has for killer sharks. As long as you see them from a distance, or on TV, that's fine—you admire their strength, their speed, their raw power. But my admiration never makes me want to swim with them in the same pool.

For the past twenty years of my life, I've been an evangelist as well. I write, I preach, I do all sorts of things to tell people about God's love.

In fact, I sometimes talk to total strangers, too.

I remember knocking on the doors of my new neighbors to give them fruits, a piece of chocolate cake, or even cookies. No preaching. No testimonies. Sometimes, I just greet them a happy morning and buzz away. Small acts of kindness. Nothing much, really.

Hopefully, if after a few days, they feel my sincere love for them, they get a tangible experience of God's sweet love—without hearing one word from me.

And perhaps, later, my neighbors may want to talk, and I'd be there to listen.

And perhaps, later still, I'd pray with them, and share my faith to them.

No, I don't want to be a shark. I'd rather be a dolphin.

Even kids love to go near dolphins—and I love kids.

It's not only more effective.

It makes my life—and my mission—immeasurably fun.

BE GOOD ADS FOR GOD

"You need to talk to my sin-infested, vice-ridden, devil-possessed husband!"

I finished preaching in a prayer meeting when this huge woman approached me and said these acidic words. She went on, "My no-good husband's here to pick me up, but can you meet him first and pray that his depraved soul doesn't go to Hell?"

"Uh, sure…" I said. During these awkward times, I end up wondering why I didn't become a plumber instead of a preacher. After fixing leaky pipes, plumbers can go home. After I preach a sermon, I can't go home. I still have to fix leaky pipes—like this woman who "leaked" all that I preached about that night on *love, humility, kindness,* etc.

"Just a moment," she said, hastily turning towards the door. In a few minutes, I saw her with her not-so-pleased husband in tow.

"Here he is, Bo!" she announced as she pulled him towards me. "He's a lazy drunkard, a gambler, a womanizer. He doesn't have the Holy Spirit! He's so far from the Lord!" I wondered when this tirade would end. Humiliating and lambasting her husband seemed to be *her* spiritual gift. I pitied the guy, who was now trying to hide his face behind the collars of his denim jacket. I swear his neck had totally shrunk, and his head was getting shorter and smaller as the minutes wore on.

Finally, I had to interrupt and greeted the man, "I'm happy that you're here. I can see you're a very caring husband for picking up your wife tonight."

From the corner of my eye, I saw his wife's shocked face glaring at me.

"Well, yes, I do care for her...," he said sheepishly.

"And I apologize for your wife's, uh, ways," I winked.

"I'm used to her," he chuckled, "she does this all the time!"

I bent over and whispered to his ear, "Let's pray that God will fill her with the Holy Spirit. She might just change, you know."

He laughed uproariously. His wife interrupted, "Brother Bo, don't talk too softly! I can't hear you!"

Her husband whispered back to me, "Is there hope for her?"

"God can change anyone," I declared, "Hey, you're invited to attend the prayer meeting next time," I smiled, "so that you could pray for your wife's transformation."

As the couple walked out of the prayer meeting hall with the man's head back to it's normal position, and his dazed wife right behind him, I began wondering. How many people don't come closer to God because of His lousy advertisements?

Hey, the "product" itself is great: Salvation, Forgiveness, Heaven, True Joy!

But God has chosen ads that are the pits: human beings called Christians.

We are appointed to advertise God to others, but we do it bizarrely. We advertise God by condemning, judging, acting self-righteously, pulling rank, boasting, and so on.

Friends, be good advertising.

God's counting on you.

Acknowledgement

Books like these are born from Communities and families, and this one is no different. It is a garment of praise that has been woven from the blessings that friends have left with me.

My children by acquisition, I love you!

My spiritual community, the LIGHT OF JESUS, my dearest friends.

My fellow elders, Pio Español, Jill Ramiscal, Toj Calaycay, Jun Fontecha—working with you is God's special gift to me.

My dedicated directors, Omec Roderos, Roy Pasimio, Hermie Morelos, Tim Duran, Eng Si, Dong Matias, Lito Saura, Banjoy Santillan, Vic and Ditas Español, Marisa Chikiamco, Tita Neneng Mangahas. His light shines through you!

My spiritual mentor, Mike Joseph, Jr.

My angels in God's work, Eliza Manaloto, Lucy Limpe, Betty Roxas-Chua, Felicitas Sy.

And our donors all over the world who believe in the mission. You are His encouragement to me.

Priests assigned to my life, Bishop Ted Bacani, Jr., D.D.; Fr. Steve Tynan, MGL;

Fr. Rudy Horst, SVD; Fr. Dong Alpuerto, SVD; Fr. Andy Biller, SVD.

My co-laborers in other vineyards of the Lord: Omy and Rosanne Romero, Jeanne Young, Jake Yap, Francis Iturralde, Ken Noecker, Pete Lapid, Sis. Angelina Lim, and Adrian Panganiban. Thank you for always having a difficult time saying no to my requests!

My fellow full-time staffers in SHEPHERD'S VOICE, ANAWIM, the LIGHT OF JESUS (LOJ) Community, the LOJ Counselling Center, and the LOJ Training Center. I thank my God for each of you.

My loving parents, Gene and Pilar. I embrace you each day.

My family: my sisters, their husbands, my nephews and nieces, and my first grandchild–hugs!

My parents-in-law, Ruben and Linda, for loving me as your favorite son-in-law.

My team in producing and distributing this book: Alma Alvarez, my excellent editor, and Tubby, the book's layout artist; editor-at-large Chay Santiago; finance whiz Weng Cequeña; sales evangelist Mon Toledo; distribution expert Bebeth Bacolod;

and admin servant Cindy Calderon. To all my friends distributing God's Word across the country and the world, He delights in you!

My wife, Marowe, for always being my best friend.

THEY NEED YOUR LOVE
Anawim: Refuge for the Poor

In June of 1996, *ANAWIM* began its full operations when an old man in dirty rags entered the bamboo gate of its rustic compound. The following week, a whole family of eight orphans arrived from the mountains. A few days later, a mother and her five children were running away from a physically abusive husband and father.

Within three years, the *ANAWIM* Center has become a refuge for twenty (20) abandoned elderly, fifteen (15) poor children, two (2) mentally handicapped persons, and countless of transients who seek for inner healing.

Anawim, a Hebrew word meaning, "the poor of the Lord" began with a simple dream of Bo Sanchez and the *Light of Jesus Community*. They wanted to love.

But giving love to the poor is costly. Feeding sixty persons each day—composed of the poor, the volunteers, the transients— is no small task. Medical bills are extremely expensive for the elderly. We spend P250,000 each month for this work of love.

Should you wish to help this work, contact or write to: *ANAWIM*, #56 Chicago St., Cubao, Quezon City 1109 Philippines. Pager #: 141-114883. *They need your love.*

AN INVITATION
TO KEEP ON GROWING

Should you wish to continue following the spiritual path explained in this book, you can read any of the inspiring publications of SHEPHERD'S VOICE or listen to the power-packed Teaching Tapes of Bo Sanchez and other speakers.

PERIODICALS:
KERYGMA, a Catholic Inspirational Magazine
DIDACHE, a Daily Bible Reflection Guide for Catholics
GABAY, Pang-araw-araw na Pagninilay para sa Katoliko
COMPANION, a Catholic Scripture Diary

TEACHING TAPES:
Build Your Throne *(1 tape)*, by Bo Sanchez
Daily Discipleship *(10 tapes)*, by Bo Sanchez
Bible Study for Catholics (*10 Tapes*), by Bo Sanchez
Loving God When He Seems Far Away (*3 tapes*), by Bo Sanchez

Spiritual Warfare *(3 tapes)*, by Bo Sanchez

Secret of Sainthood *(2 tapes)*, by Bo Sanchez

Holy Rosary *(3 tapes)*, by Bo Sanchez

The Way of the Cross *(1 tape)*, by Bo Sanchez

Tape of the Month Specials, by Bo Sanchez

Introduction to the Christian Family Life *(3 tapes)*, by Pio Español

God in the Desert *(1 tape)*, by Rosanne Romero

If you are interested in any of these products, contact us at the address or numbers below. God bless you.

SHEPHERD'S VOICE
#60 Chicago St., Cubao
Quezon City 1109 Philippines
Tel. No. (02) 411-7874
Fax No. (02) 727-5615
E-mail: sale-svp@philonline.com.ph

Dear Reader,

I pray that this special collection has blessed your life and drew you closer to God. It was a thrill writing these stories for you.

If you wish to send me a message, my e-mail address is bomarowe@info.com.ph Because of the amount of mail we receive, I may not be able to respond to you. But I do promise to read your message.

We have a prayer hot-line. If you have any prayer requests, e-mail us at praybox@philonline.com.ph and we will be glad to pray for you. You can also mail us at our home office at SHEPHERD'S VOICE, c/o praybox, #60 Chicago St., Cubao, Quezon City 1109 Philippines, or call us at Tel. No. (02) 411-7874.

Aside from the publications and teaching tapes we produce at SHEPHERD'S VOICE, I also hold seminars through the LIGHT OF JESUS TRAINING CENTER, INC. I hope to see you in one of them.

May His love always be the fire in your heart.

I remain your friend,

ABOUT THE AUTHOR:

Bo Sanchez is the founder of ANAWIM, a special ministry for the poor, providing a home for the abandoned elderly and a few children. He also  established SHEPHERD'S VOICE Publications, a media ministry that publishes one of the widest read Catholic literature in the Philippines. He also organized the LIGHT OF JESUS TRAINING CENTER, a teaching institute whose mission is to impart truth through seminars and workshops all over the country. He also pioneered the LIGHT OF JESUS Community, an organization of lay Catholics from where was born the LIGHT OF JESUS Counseling Center. Bo began preaching at the age of thirteen and hasn't stopped ever since. He lives with his wife, Marowe, and son, Benedict Thomas, in Manila, Philippines.

YOU CAN MAKE YOUR LIFE BEAUTIFUL

This beautiful book about making life beautiful is a second collection of *The BOss* articles from *KERYGMA*, and nationally known author and speaker Bo Sanchez will do what he is best known for: From his heart to yours, he shares common stories with uncommon wisdom. Join him in his personal journeys of deep faith and tender love, and your heart will overflow with laughter and warmth.

This special collection includes the most favorite of Bo's articles, such as...

Give Your Heart Away & Find It Whole
Avoid Potholes By Taking Humps
Nurture Your Secret Life
The Fastest Guy Doesn't Win the Race
Wipe While Wet
Only Love Heals

This book can profoundly change the way you look at life.